5 Top Phonics Readers

# When They Are Big

Anne Taylor

Seed Learning

# Top Phonics Readers 5
## When They Are Big
Anne Taylor

© 2017 Seed Learning, Inc.

Acquisitions Editor: Rose Morgan
Content Editor: Liana Robinson
Illustrators: Story 1 - Jillian Altmeyer; Story 2 - Conor Rawson;
            Story 3 - Genie Espinosa; Story 4 - James Murray
Design: Highline Studio

http://www.seed-learning.com

ISBN: 978-1-9464-5277-1

10 9 8 7 6 5 4 3 2 1
21 20 19 18 17

# Contents

# A Train Ride

## -ai-, -ar-, -ay-, -or-

Written by **Anne Taylor**
Illustrated by **Jillian Altmeyer**

The mail comes.
"This is for you," says Dad.
It has big red stars.
What is it?

It is a card.
There is a train on the card.
It is a prize.
Two tickets for the train!

Robbie and Dad use their tickets.
They don't pay!
A man gives Robbie crayons.
But Robbie doesn't want to draw.

Robbie can see many things
from the train.
He sees some cars.
They are slow!

Robbie sees the park.
Kids are playing.
He waves both of his arms.
"Hello! I'm on the train!"

It starts to rain.
Robbie sees a farm.
There is a white ram with big horns.
There is a black horse.

Robbie sees corn.
Lots and lots of corn!
"Dad, can we make popcorn tonight?"

# By the Sea

**-ea-, -ee-, -oa-, -ow**

Written by **Anne Taylor**
Illustrated by **Conor Rawson**

Bee brings a green leaf and a pillow.
He flies above the road.
"Where are you going?" ask the geese.
"To the beach," says Bee.

"Can we come?" ask the geese.
"Yes. But bring some tea and some toast."
The geese bring tea and toast.

Bee and the geese go along the road.
Goat looks out his window.
"Can I come?" asks Goat.
"Yes, but bring some seeds," says Bee.

"Look! The sea! We are at the beach."
There is a boat. They get on the boat.
Bee uses his leaf and his pillow.
He makes a nice seat.

Goat rows the boat away from the beach.
The geese throw many yellow seeds into
the sea.
Soon they have many fish friends.

"I'm hungry. Can we have tea and toast?"
asks Goat.
"Yes," says Bee.
Bee, the geese, and Goat start to eat.

Goat is very hungry.
He eats the green leaf.
He eats Bee's pillow.
"Goat!" says Bee.

# What's So Loud?

-ou-, -ow-, -oy, -oi-

Written by **Anne Taylor**
Illustrated by **Genie Espinosa**

What is that?
It's too loud!

Is it that Mouse in her house?
She likes to play her drum.
Bang, bang, bang!
No, it's not the mouse.

Is it Roy with his toys?
Roy sings with joy when he plays.
He can be such a loud boy!
No, it's not Roy.

Is it that clown with a big red mouth?
The clown likes to count balls.
Some balls can fall.
No, it's not the clown.

Is it the oil?
Mom boils oil to cook some soy.
Pop! Pop! Pop!
No, it's not the oil.

Is it that king with a crown?
The king wears a crown and
rides a cow.
No, it's not the king.

It's the rain from a cloud.
The rain hits the soil.
It's very loud!

# When They Are Big

### long -oo-, short -oo-, -er-, -ir-, -ur-

Written by Anne Taylor

Illustrated by James Murray

Ken likes to cook.
He has a big spoon.
His spoon is made of wood.
He uses his spoon to stir.

When he is big, Ken will be a baker.
He will make birthday cakes for kids.

Dan likes to read books.
He likes to look at the moon and the stars.
When he is big, he will go to the moon.

Tina likes to play soccer.
She likes to swim and surf.
When she is big, she will have a pool.

Robbie likes to be with animals.
He has a goose and a ram.
When he is big, he will work at a zoo.

Anna likes to dance.
She likes to take care of her toys, too.
When she is big, she will be a dancer
or a nurse. She does not know yet!

A dancer, a baker, a nurse?
Will you work on the moon or in a zoo?
What will you be when you are big?

# Word List

## Story 1

mail

rain

train

crayon

pay

say

arm

car

card

farm

park

star

corn

horn

horse

## Story 2

bee

geese

green

seed

beach

eat

leaf

sea

seat

tea

boat

goat

road

toast

pillow

row

throw

window

yellow

# Word List

## Story 3

b**oil**

**oil**

s**oil**

b**oy**

j**oy**

R**oy**

s**oy**

t**oy**

cl**ow**n

c**ow**

cr**ow**n

cl**ou**d

c**ou**nt

h**ou**se

l**ou**d

m**ou**se

m**ou**th

## Story 4

bak**er**

danc**er**

socc**er**

b**ir**thday

st**ir**

n**ur**se

s**ur**f

g**oo**se

m**oo**n

p**oo**l

sp**oo**n

z**oo**

b**oo**k

c**oo**k

l**oo**k

w**oo**d

# How to Use

The following are some ideas for ways to use the stories in this book.

## Idea 1

★ Choose a story.
★ Look at the **Word List** for that story.
★ Find each word from the list in the story.
★ Then read the story.

## Idea 2

★ Choose a story.
★ Look at the illustrations for the story.
★ Talk about the illustrations: Point and say the words you know in the illustrations.
★ Look for the words from the illustrations in the story while you read.

## Idea 3

★ Choose a story.
★ Look at all the words with red letters in the story. Circle the words you know.
★ If you don't know a word, check the **Word List**.
★ Then read the story.
★ After reading, look at the words again. Can you remember the meaning of each one?

## Idea 4

★ Choose a story.
★ Look at the illustration on each page: What do you see? What is happening?
★ Guess what you think the page will say.
★ Then read the page.
★ Repeat for every page of the story.